MARC ELLIS SCARFIES COOKBOOK

MARC

SCARFiES
COOKBOOK

ELLiS

MARC ELLIS

SCARFIES COOKBOOK

Hodder Moa Beckett

Sponsors

DOLMIO and MASTERFOODS are proud to be associated with the publication of Marc Ellis's *Scarfies Cookbook*. With the following recipes, creating exciting, interesting meals has never been so easy and we are delighted to have Marc promoting our products.

ISBN 1-86958-582-8

© 1997 text MCG Marketing Ltd
© 1997 recipes Hodder Moa Beckett and Effem Foods Ltd
© photographs Hodder Moa Beckett

MASTERFOODS, DOLMIO, PRIMA and UNCLE BEN'S are
registered trademarks © Effem Foods Ltd, 1997

Published in 1997 by Hodder Moa Beckett Publishers Limited
[a member of the Hodder Headline Group]
4 Whetu Place, Mairangi Bay, Auckland, New Zealand

Designed, typeset and produced by Hodder Moa Beckett Publishers Limited

Cover and inside photographs: Sally Tagg
Cooking equipment and clothing supplied by The House of Knives, Auckland

Printed by Colorcraft, Hong Kong

CONTENTS

Introduction

This book has been designed to eliminate any potential embarrassment that can, and does, occur in the kitchen on a regular basis. The recipes are based on proven student delights, easily prepared and consumed. Sometimes convenience foods are the order of the day when you want to prepare a quick meal. But often, being a student of limited means means you have to think quite laterally in terms of catering for your next meal. A few classic examples spring to mind.

One mate (who will obviously remain nameless) lived right on the main Leith River running through Otago University. Ducks often congregated in his back garden. This cobber took to feeding them breadcrumbs and by mid-winter, with a cunning trail of breadcrumbs, was able to entice them all into the kitchen where he was waiting behind the door. Suffice to say, that cold winter evening the flat ate very well.

The same chap got a fair bit of ribbing about turning into a pansy when he bought himself a butterfly net. It wasn't until he was seen scooping salmon out of the Leith River that his masculinity was truly restored. Further to this he had the audacity to invite his department head around to dine on his catch in an attempt to influence his exam results. He finished his degree that year.

Both of the above efforts were heavily fined offences and were looked upon in such a light by the university that they would not hesitate to offer the student to the authorities. I wonder what would have happened to the head of department?

For my 21st I was gifted a small pig by a mate. The very same evening after returning home by taxi and feeling no small amount of compassion for my new companion I turned my pig loose in my bedroom. I was then woken in the early hours of the morning by the pig trying to get under the covers having feasted on an exquisitely prepared 21st cake. After this he was tied to the clothesline. Winter, however, took its toll and the now half-grown pig was allowed inside again. This time he had his own room – the bathroom! He lasted there a whole week due to a democratic vote (4 guys – 3 girls) before he was finally sent off to a fattening farm. They're not the sort of animals you keep inside. You will by now be getting a feeling for the esteem in which food is held in a university flat. It is a great idea to flat with someone from a farming background.

Another favourite with my group of mates was known as the 'Castle St mile'. This took place after a night of merriment at the Gardies tavern at the top of Castle St. You needed to prepare for this by borrowing a sack or large bag from the pub. The group would then hare off down Castle St raiding every flat on the left and the right and throwing all the meat from

the freezers into the sack. The record to the best of my knowledge stands at 6.40 mins, 8 chickens, 7kg steak, a winter's worth of mince and sausages, 1 lemon and a cucumber. This would be done late on a Monday evening as shopping day for the majority of flats was usually around this time.

The Cadbury's tour (with its free chocolate), supermarket tastings (often started by over zealous students) and honesty boxes (which often didn't live up to their names) were other favourites.

The Speights tour was probably the most widely utilised option for free food. After a tantalising 40 minute tour members of the public were invited to the boardroom where they were offered some of this fine product to taste. After 3 or 4 tours you certainly knew all there was to know so an early exit to the boardroom was attempted. The record for this early indulgence was 7 1/2 jugs (if this has been bettered please let me know). One mate from Murdoch was so perturbed when the guide failed to show one day that he led the public through the first 20 mins of the tour before the guide showed up.

May I take this opportunity to apologise to my uni flatmates who endured some culinary disasters as a result of our financial hardship and a vivid imagination. Some of the unique recipes enclosed would not have found these pages otherwise.

Marc Ellis

Getting

Obviously it is prudent to start on the basics and work your way up to more

complicated delights. Hence this very quick and convenient section to knock your hunger over in as little time as possible.

Started

BOILED EGGS

1-2 eggs per serve
Cold water

1. Put eggs in small pot and cover with water.
2. Bring water to the boil, reduce heat to medium and take note of the time:
   - For soft-boiled eggs with runny yolks, cook 2 mins more;
   - Medium-soft yolks, cook 4 mins more;
   - Hard yolks, cook 6 mins more.
3. Remove pot from heat immediately and drain eggs. If using cold, such as for salads, run water from cold tap over eggs briefly, otherwise put in eggcups and serve immediately.

HINT: Have the eggs at room temperature to avoid them cracking in the pot. If they do show signs of cracking, put 2 T vinegar in the water. This will seal the shells and set any egg white which may have escaped.

POACHED EGGS

2 eggs (preferably at room temp.) per serve
Cold water
Salt

1. In shallow pan half filled, bring water to boil and add salt.
2. Carefully break each egg into a saucer before sliding into the water. Cook for 3-4 mins. Do not allow water to boil fast or eggs will become tough. Ladle water over yolks if you want an evenly cooked egg.
3. Remove eggs with spatula. Serve on toast.

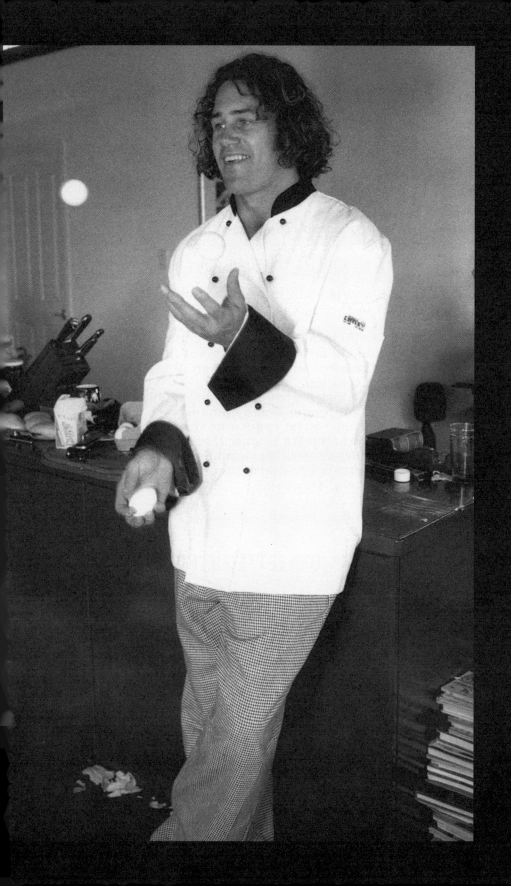

OMELETTE

2 eggs
2 T cold water
Salt and pepper
Butter
Fillings if desired (see below)

1. With a fork whisk together eggs, water and seasonings.
2. Heat omelette pan thoroughly and melt enough butter to thickly coat sides and bottom. Reduce heat slightly.
3. Tip in egg mixture and swirl around sides of pan. Cook quickly until it starts to set, keeping mixture moving in base and shaking pan occasionally to prevent sticking.
4. For plain omelette: reduce heat, fold in half, remove to warm plate and serve immediately.
5. For filled omelette: reduce heat, spoon desired filling on half of omelette in pan, then cover this by folding over the other half. Once filling is heated through, tip omelette on to warmed plate and serve immediately. Serves 1.

OMELETTE FILLINGS

Cheese, grated
Onion, grated – 2 T per serve, mixed with grated cheese
Chopped parsley or other herbs, e.g. chives, rocket, basil, chervil, dill, etc. – 2 T per serve
Diced ham, salami, cooked chicken or fried bacon
**   – 1/2 cup per serve**
Sautéed mushrooms – 1/2 cup per serve
Flaked cooked salmon or tuna – 1/2 cup per serve

HEARTY GOURMET OMELETTE

2 T olive oil
250g precooked sausages, sliced thinly
2 rashers bacon, chopped
2 potatoes, peeled and chopped
8 eggs
2 t MASTERFOODS omelette herbs
1/4 t MASTERFOODS cracked black peppercorns

1. Heat oil in a large frying pan. Sauté sausage and bacon until bacon is crisp. Remove to plate.
2. Add potatoes to same pan. Sauté until golden and tender.
3. Whisk together eggs, omelette herbs and cracked black peppercorns.
4. Stir the sausage and bacon mixture into the egg mixture. Pour into pan. Cook for 2-3 mins or until beginning to set. Turn to cook the other side. Cut in a wedge to serve. Serves 4.

OMELETTE FILLINGS

Smoked fish in white sauce – 1/2 cup per serve
Mussels, oysters, prawns or shrimps, all prepared and pre-cooked by usual methods – 1/2 cup per serve
Mixed diced and cooked vegetables, seasoned and herbed
Sliced fresh tomatoes and chopped basil
Sliced sautéed capsicum and courgettes with mixed herbs
Cooked asparagus tips with cheese sauce
Cooked kernel or creamed sweetcorn

CREAMY SCRAMBLED EGGS

2 eggs
2 T cream or milk
25g butter
Salt and pepper

1. With a fork beat together eggs and cream or milk in a bowl until well combined.
2. Melt butter in shallow pan and reduce heat before it browns.
3. Season egg mixture and pour into pan. Stirring gently, cook until mixture is stiff but still creamy.
4. Remove pan from heat and pile contents on to toast. Serves 1.

EGG COMBO

2 T butter
1/2 cup ham, shredded
1/2 capsicum, finely diced
6 eggs, lightly beaten with 4 T milk
1/2 cup grated cheese, tightly packed
2 t **MASTERFOODS** chives
1 t **MASTERFOODS** seasoned pepper
1/4 t **MASTERFOODS** paprika to garnish
Toast

1. Melt butter in large pan.
2. Add ham and capsicum and cook over high heat for 2-3 mins.
3. Add lightly beaten eggs and milk, cheese, **MASTERFOODS** chives and seasoned pepper.
4. Combine lightly in pan.
5. Place lid on pan and cook gently for 5 mins or until eggs are set.
6. Sprinkle with paprika to serve and accompany with hot buttered toast fingers. Serves 2-3.

SCARFIES FRENCH TOAST

6 eggs
6 T milk
6 slices brown or white bread
6 t butter

1. Beat eggs with milk until well mixed but not frothy.
2. Dip sliced bread into this mixture, turning to moisten both sides.
3. Leave coated bread to stand on flat plate for several minutes before cooking in a moderately hot buttered pan, allowing about half a teaspoon of butter for each side.
4. Cook long enough to brown evenly on both sides.
5. Serve hot with honey, maple or golden syrup, jam and bananas.

For savoury French toast serve with sautéed sliced tomatoes, mushrooms, or creamed corn.

GOURMET CHEESE ON TOAST

1 T DOLMIO PRIMA Pesto with sundried tomatoes
1 slice toast
1 slice ham
1 slice cheese
1 ring pineapple, well drained
1 egg, separated
Sprinkling MASTERFOODS paprika
Grated cheese

1. Preheat oven at 180°C for 10 mins.
2. Spread half the pesto over toast.
3. Layer ham, cheese, pineapple on to toast and spread remaining pesto over pineapple. Place on baking tray.
4. Stiffly beat egg white, fold in yolk and paprika.
5. Spoon over toast and sprinkle with cheese.
6. Bake for 10-15 mins or until puffed and golden.
7. Serve immediately. Serves 1.

CAPSICUM 'N' CHEESE TOASTED SANDWICH

2 slices bread
2 T DOLMIO PRIMA pesto with roasted capsicum
2 slices cheese
1 slice meat of choice (ham, beef, luncheon
   sausage, salami)
2 olives or gherkins

1. Spread each slice of bread with pesto.
2. Place a slice of cheese on each and spread any
   remaining pesto on to one slice and top with meat
   and remaining slices of cheese and bread.
3. Toast on both sides under the grill or in a toasted
   sandwich maker.
4. Spear olive or gherkin onto a toothpick and use as a
   garnish.

SEAFARERS SPREAD

1 x 425g can tuna in brine, well drained
1 x T MASTERFOODS dill leaf tips
1 x 165g jar PRIMA DOLMIO Pesto with sundried
   tomatoes

1. Combine ingredients in a bowl.
2. Use to spread on sandwiches, then top with salad
   ingredients of your choice.

MIGHTY MEAT SANDWICH

1 T DOLMIO PRIMA Pesto roasted capsicum
1 t MASTERFOODS Hot English or Dijon mustard
2 slices toast-thickness bread
2-4 slices rare roast beef
4 thin slices tomatoes
Shredded lettuce or alfalfa sprouts and other salad
   ingredients of choice

1. Combine DOLMIO PRIMA pesto and mustard and
   spread over bread.
2. Top 1 slice with beef and salad ingredients and
   finally remaining slice of bread.
3. Cut in half and serve or cover and refrigerate until
   required.

Variation: Use chicken or roast pork

MORE TOASTED SANDWICH FILLINGS

MASTERFOODS Mexican Chilli beans and diced fried bacon with grated cheese

Mushrooms sautéed with MASTERFOODS mixed herbs, alfalfa sprouts and shredded ham

Diced cooked chicken, mashed banana and mango pickle

Shaved ham, crushed pineapple and grated cheese

Fried egg, diced cooked bacon and tomato sauce

Leftover roast meat slices – beef, ham, lamb, pork or poultry – with appropriate condiments and pickles, e.g. horseradish, mustard, cranberry, apple or plum sauce, mint jelly – and salad stuffs: lettuce, sprouts, tomato slices, gherkins, olives, etc.

Diced cooked chicken, diced fresh apple, walnuts and chutney

Mashed asparagus with herbed sour cream or grated cheese

Mixed bean sprouts and shredded cooked omelette with chopped almonds

Blue cheese, grapes and fresh pear slices

Fried onion rings, fresh sliced tomatoes and grated cheese

Diced cooked vegetables with herbs and grated cheese

Red onion rings, chopped cooked mussels and cheese

Sliced cooked salmon, cream cheese and gherkins

Cooked chopped oysters in white sauce with bacon bits

Mashed sardines, pesto and tomato slices

Flaked tuna with diced fresh capsicum and tomato slices

CHICKEN AND GHERKIN DELIGHT

Shredded smoked chicken
MASTERFOODS gherkin relish
Low-fat sour cream
MASTERFOODS lemon pepper seasoning
Lettuce
Tomato slices
Grated cheese

1. Combine first four ingredients and spread on sandwich bread, crusty rolls, pita or crispbreads.
2. Top with salad ingedients.

GREEN AND GOLD SANDWICH

Coarsely chopped walnuts
4 T cream cheese
1 T mayonnaise
Chopped dried dessert apricots
2 slices brown or wholegrain bread
1 slice white bread, buttered
Cooked mashed asparagus
Salt and pepper
1/4 t MASTERFOODS paprika to garnish

1. Combine first 4 ingredients to make a thick spread and divide between 2 slices of brown bread.
2. Layer as follows:
   brown bread slice with walnut/apricot mixture
   white buttered slice
   thick layer of seasoned asparagus
   inverted brown slice
3. Cut into half diagonally.

HAMBURGER WITH THE WORKS

1/2 cup breadcrumbs
400g lean beef
1 egg
1 T MASTERFOODS italian herbs
4 hamburger buns, grilled and buttered
1 cup shredded lettuce
2 tomatoes, sliced
4 beetroot slices
4 rashers bacon, grilled
4 slices processed cheese
1/2 cup MASTERFOODS mild chunky salsa

1. Combine first 4 ingredients and form into patties.
2. Grill or pan fry patties until cooked through.
3. Place a patty in each bun and then fill with
   remaining ingredients. Serves 4.

PESTO DOGS

6 sausages (beef, frankfurter, pork, etc.)
1 large onion, thinly sliced
Oil of your choice
1 x 165g jar DOLMIO PRIMA Pesto with roasted
    capsicum
MASTERFOODS mustard of choice to taste
    (e.g. wholegrain, mild)
6 hot dog rolls or long pieces French bread

1. Grill or BBQ sausages (reheat leftover cooked
   sausages).
2. While meat is grilling, stirfry onion in a little oil until
   brown and cooked.
3. Stir in 2 T pesto and keep warm until required.
4. Combine remaining pesto with mustard.
5. Split rolls, leaving them hinged, and spread with
   pesto mustard.
6. Place a cooked sausage in each roll and serve at
   once topped with onions. Serves 3.

TACOS

1 x 420g tin of MASTERFOODS Mexican chilli beans
8 Tacos shells (heat in oven following packet
    directions)
Grated cheese
Shredded lettuce
1 cup grated cheddar cheese
Chopped spring onions (or onion rings)
Sour cream
Extra MASTERFOODS Sweet Thai chilli sauce
    (for those who like it hot and spicy)
2 avocados, peeled and sliced (optional)

1. Heat Mexican chilli beans.
2. Fill tacos with chilli beans.
3. Add remaining ingredients on top. Serves 4.

PiTA POCKETS

Pita pockets are halved breads which can be tidily filled with just about anything (and everything, if you use the larger size). All the sandwich combos on p. 21-24 will fit into pita pockets, and many others too. Refried beans, beansprouts, green salad, tabouleh, tahini, thick yoghurt, sour cream, cottage cheese and meats thinly sliced or generously chunked are all traditional ingredients which can be successfully packed into pockets of pita.

Pita also make excellent bases for pizza, maxi or mini sized. Spread each side with butter, margarine or good olive oil and toast, fry lightly in large pan, crisp under a grill or just heat 20-35 seconds in a microwave oven. Assemble your pita pizza as on p. 64-5, using plenty of Italian tomato herbed sauce, grated cheese and any toppings which may be in the fridge. Bake or grill till heated.

Pita stacks are slightly more time-consuming than your ordinary sandwich but make spectacular study fare. After crisping up each pita as directed for pizza, carefully slit round enough of the side of each flat bread to let you push in selected sandwich fillings. Spread butter, mayonnaise or appropriate sauce on the tops of 2 filled pita and stack up the rounds in 3s, with an unbuttered filled pita on top. Quarter each pita stack by twice slicing through vertically with a sharp knife. To eat, pull apart the wedges, which will look (and taste) best if you've contrasted your fillings, club-sandwich style.

NACHOS

1 packet nachos
1 x 420g tin MASTERFOODS Mexican chilli beans
Grated cheese
Sour cream

1. Layer nachos on a flat baking dish or tray.
2. Add Mexican chilli beans.
3. Sprinkle grated cheese on top.
4. Bake in oven at 180°C until beans are hot and cheese has melted (Optional: turn oven on to grill and grill until cheese turns golden brown).
5. Add sour cream on top.

BLACK PUDDING

Being a much-loved food of mine, a few tips on how to obtain a good pud and how best to cook it.

My preference is to go to the local quality butcher and have them prepare a Black Pudding for you. This cuts down the preservative content and also insures you have the fresh option.

First, skin your black pudding, then slice down the middle making two halves.

When cooking, melt butter and gently fry until the exterior is golden brown while not dry inside.

One-Pot

Experimentation is the key word for developing one-pot wonders. Never throw away left-over food (a golden rule as a scarfie). In fact, some of

the greatest meals are born through combining left-over tucker in a pot or pan. Don't be shy, it's amazing what can, and will, taste good together!

Wonders

MARC'S SHANK SOUP

1 big boil-up pot
1 1/2 kg bacon bones (any bones will do as a base,
    e.g. mutton, beef)
6 carrots, chopped
3 onions, chopped
8 large potatoes, diced
3 celery sticks, diced, add leaves for flavour
1 large pkt mixed soup mix
Tabasco sauce, salt and pepper to taste

1. Boil bones over low heat overnight (watch water
   levels).
2. Remove bones and the meat should fall off to
   complete stock.
3. Skim off excess fat when cool.
4. Add fresh vegetables and boil for 90 mins until
   vegetables are soft.
5. Add soup mix and simmer for a further 90 mins.
6. Season to taste.

MINESTRONE

1 cup bacon pieces, chopped
1 large onion, finely chopped
1 t MASTERFOODS garlic powder
1 large potato, peeled and diced
1 large carrot, peeled and diced
1 x 420g can MASTERFOODS red kidney beans
1/2 cup beef stock
1/2 t salt
2 t MASTERFOODS italian herbs
1 t MASTERFOODS ground black pepper
4 T tomato paste
1 x 400g can tomato pieces, with liquid

1. In a large saucepan cook bacon and onion over low
   heat until golden brown.
2. Add remaining ingredients and simmer, covered, for
   90 mins.
3. Serve soup with garlic bread and a sprinkling of
   fresh parmesan cheese. Serves 3-4.

STIR FRY SWEET 'N' SOUR PORK

2 T olive oil
400–500g lean diced pork
1 x 575g jar KAN TONG sweet 'n' sour sauce with
     vegetables
2 sachets UNCLE BEN'S Boil–in–Bag rice

1. Stirfry lean diced pork in hot oil until meat is browned.
2. Add contents of sauce jar and stirfry until the mixture is heated through.
3. Serve on **UNCLE BEN'S** rice. Serves 4.

PORK WITH SPICY PLUM SAUCE

Oil for frying
400g–500g of lean pork steaks
1 x 575g jar KAN TONG spicy plum sauce with
     vegetables
2 sachets UNCLE BEN'S Boil–in–Bag rice

1. Slice pork steaks into thin strips.
2. Stirfry the strips of pork in hot oil until meat browns.
3. Add contents of jar and stirfry until the sauce is heated through.
4. Serve with UNCLE BEN'S rice. Serves 4.

SPAGHETTI BOLOGNESE

2 T olive oil
500g lean minced beef
1 onion cut into thin wedges
1 575g jar **DOLMIO** tomato, onion
   and garlic bolognese sauce
400g spaghetti

1. Heat oil in large saucepan.
2. Add onion and cook until tender.
3. Add beef and cook until brown.
4. Add jar of DOLMIO and heat through, about 10 mins.
5. Cook spaghetti as directed on packet and drain well.
6. Stir sauce into spaghetti and serve with crusty French bread. Serves 4.

CHILLI CON CARNE

1 T olive oil
1 onion, finely chopped
1/4 t **MASTERFOODS** granulated garlic
500g minced lean beef
1/2 green pepper, seeded and chopped
1 x 420g can **MASTERFOODS** red kidney beans,
   drained
4 ripe tomatoes, peeled and chopped
2 T tomato paste
1/2 t **MASTERFOODS** ground chilli
1/2 t **MASTERFOODS** oregano
1 cup beef stock
MASTERFOODS corn relish
French bread

1. Heat oil in frying pan. Add onion and cook over medium heat for 5 minutes until lightly browned.
2. Add garlic and meat and fry, stirring constantly with a fork, until cooked.
3. Add remaining ingredients, except for relish. Cover and simmer for 45 mins stirring occasionally.
4. Uncover and simmer for a further 20 mins to make a thick sauce. Taste for seasoning. Add extra chilli powder if desired.
5. Serve with salad, MASTERFOODS corn relish and crusty bread. Serves 4.

TUNA TAGLIATELLE

35g butter
1 x 185g tin tuna in oil
2 T finely chopped parsley
200ml cream
Salt and pepper
200g tagliatelle (or fettucine)

1. Heat butter in pan till melted.
2. Add chunked tuna, with its oil, and parsley. Cook gently over low heat for 5 mins.
3. Stir in cream slowly, then add seasonings and simmer, covered, for another 4–5 mins, taking care the mixture does not boil.
4. Cook tagliatelle in boiling salted water until al denté. Drain thoroughly.
5. Mix the tuna sauce through the pasta, preferably using 2 wooden forks or spoons, until well blended. Serve immediately. Serves 2.

CREAMY FETTUCINI

400g fresh fettucini
1 x 370g jar DOLMIO PRIMA fresh cream
   and sweet basil pasta sauce
2 tomatoes
125g shaved ham
2 T chopped basil leaves

1. Cook fettucini to packet directions.
2. Drain well and toss through DOLMIO PRIMA pasta sauce.
3. Chop tomatoes and arrange tomatoes and shaved ham over fettucini.
4. Sprinkle with basil. Serve immediately. Serves 4.

PESTO PENNE

250g penne pasta
250g strips vegetables, e.g. carrot, leek,
   capsicum, courgette
1 x 165g jar **DOLMIO PRIMA** pesto
   with basil, cheese and pinenuts
1/4 cup sour cream or cream
1 cup coarsely grated parmesan cheese

1. Cook pasta as directed on packet, drain and return
   to saucepan.
2. Steam or microwave vegetables until just cooked.
3. To the pasta add vegetables, pesto sauce and cream.
4. Toss gently to combine.
5. Heat and serve sprinkled with cheese. Serves 3.

TOMATO CHICKEN CONCHIGLIE

2 T oil
1 large onion, finely chopped
1 clove garlic, crushed
3 rashers streaky bacon, chopped
400g fresh tomatoes, skinned and chopped
Salt and pepper
1/2 t **MASTERFOODS** sweet basil leaves
15g butter
200g chicken livers, skinned and chopped
400g conchiglie (pasta seashells)
12g butter

1. Sauté onion, garlic and bacon in oil over medium heat
   for 5 mins.
2. Add to this the tomatoes and seasonings. Break up
   tomatoes and simmer, uncovered, for 15-20 mins.
3. In a frying pan melt the butter and sauté the chicken
   livers for 3-4 mins.
4. Mix the chicken livers into the sauce and simmer this
   mixture just enough to heat it through - 2 mins.
5. Cook the pasta shells in plenty of boiling salted water
   until al denté. Drain. Return to pan and toss in the
   second measure of butter. Divide pasta into 2-3 dishes,
   spoon over sauce and serve immediately. Serves 2-3.

PORK & KUMARA CURRY

4 kumara
3 T olive oil
400g pork steaks, cubed
1 T **MASTERFOODS** freshly crushed garlic
2 T soy sauce
1 T lemon juice
1 x 360g jar **KAN TONG** Thai red curry
100g green beans
2 sachets **UNCLE BEN'S** Boil-in-Bag rice

1. Peel kumara and simmer in boiling water until soft (or microwave on high for 10 mins). Cut into 2cm cubes.
2. Heat oil in a wok until hot.
3. Add the pork and kumara and stirfry until browned.
4. Add the KAN TONG Thai red curry, soy sauce and lemon juice and mix well.
5. Add beans and simmer until beans are hot.
6. Serve immediately on **UNCLE BEN'S** rice. Serves 4.

EASY THAI GREEN CHICKEN CURRY

2 T oil
1/2 onion, finely chopped
500g chicken, diced
1 x 360g jar **KAN TONG** Thai green curry
2 sachets **UNCLE BEN'S** Boil-in-Bag rice

1. Heat oil in wok or fry pan.
2. Add onions and sauté until golden brown.
3. Add chicken and stirfry until cooked.
4. Pour over jar of KAN TONG Thai green curry, and heat through.
5. Serve over **UNCLE BEN'S** Boil-in-Bag rice, cooked as directed on packet. Serves 4.

CHINESE MEATBALLS

1 onion, grated
25g butter, melted
2 large stalks celery, chopped finely
2 rashers bacon, diced
1 1/2 cups flour, sifted
2 eggs, beaten till frothy
2 cups finely shredded cabbage
450g minced pork
4 T finely chopped red or green capsicum
2 T soy sauce
Freshly ground black pepper
Oil for frying
2 sachets UNCLE BEN'S Boil-in-Bag rice

1. Sauté onion in butter.
2. Add celery and bacon and cook till tender.
3. Combine the above with remaining ingredients.
4. With floured hands, roll the mixture into balls and coat these in extra flour.
5. Fry meatballs in hot oil until golden and cooked through.
6. Serve with UNCLE BEN's hot rice. Serves 4.

CAJUN SAUSAGE CASSEROLE

2 T oil
500g sausage meat (preferably beef)
1 medium onion, grated
2 small carrots, grated
1/2 capsicum, finely diced
2 t MASTERFOODS cajun seasoning
1 packet (29g) oxtail soup mix
500ml cold water
500g potatoes, peeled and cubed

1. Heat oil in heavy casserole dish.
2. Combine meat, onion, carrot, capsicum and cajun seasoning. Form this sausage mix into squares and brown in hot oil. Pour off fat and set aside meat to drain on kitchen paper.
4. In pan put water and soup mix. Whisk well to combine, then stir in potatoes. Add meat patties and simmer this mixture, covered in foil, until potatoes are just cooked. Serves 4.

ORIENTAL LAMB

2 T olive oil
1 onion, cut into eighths
500g lean lamb, sliced
1/2 cup red wine
2 T soy sauce
1 T dry sherry
2 T MASTERFOODS sweet chilli sauce
1 T MASTERFOODS ground ginger
1 T sesame oil
1/2 t MASTERFOODS Chinese five spice
6 shallots, sliced
2 sachets UNCLE BEN'S Boil-in-Bag rice

1. Heat oil in a wok. Add onion. Stirfry for 1 min.
2. Mix in lamb. Stirfry for 2-3 mins.
3. Pour over combined wine, soy sauce, sweet chilli sauce, ground ginger and Chinese five spice. Stirfry until boiling.
4. Toss through shallots.
5. Serve immediately with **UNCLE BEN'S** rice. Serves 4.

STIR FRY RICE

2 T oil
3 cups cooked UNCLE BEN'S rice
2 T MASTERFOODS stirfry seasoning
1/2 cup chopped red pepper
1/2 cup chopped spring onion
1 egg

1. Heat oil in wok or fry pan.
2. Add rice, seasoning and vegetables, stirring constantly, until rice begins to brown.
3. Add egg and gently stir through, until egg is cooked.
4. Serve hot. Serves 3-4.

CURRY RICE

2 cups UNCLE BEN'S cooked rice
2 T MASTERFOODS Madras curry powder
Dried apricots, chopped
Sultanas

Cook rice as per packet directions, add seasoning and dried fruit and mix well. Serves 2-3.

TANDOORI RICE

2 bags UNCLE BEN'S Boil-in-Bag rice
2 T Tandoori seasoning
Currants
Shredded coconut

Cook rice as per packet directions, add seasoning and remaining ingredients and mix well.

BEAN & BEEF HOTPOT

2 T olive oil
2 onions, finely sliced
2 T MASTERFOODS garlic granules
1 kilo beef, such as rump or topside, cubed
1/2 cup red wine
2 T MASTERFOODS parsley flakes
1 x 440g can MASTERFOODS red kidney beans,
    drained
1 x 300 jar MASTERFOODS hot chunky salsa

1. In a large, heavy-based pan, heat oil, add onions
    and cook, stirring, 4–5 mins.
2. Add beef and garlic and cook, stirring 5–6 mins until
    brown.
3. Add wine and parsley.
4. Put lid on pan and cook on low for 1 hour.
5. Add kidney beans and salsa and cook for a further
    30–35 mins.
6. Serve hot. Serves 6.

BEEF STROGANOFF

2 T olive oil
375g sirloin steak, trimmed and cubed
Freshly ground black pepper
1 small onion, chopped
1 clove garlic, crushed
2 cups sliced mushrooms
1/2 cup chicken stock
1 t MASTERFOODS ground paprika
3/4 cup sour cream
1 t MASTERFOODS dill leaf tips

1. In large heavy-based pan heat oil. Add steak and black pepper and fry over medium heat until meat is well browned (2-3 mins). Remove meat to a plate.
2. In same pan over medium heat cook onion and garlic briefly, then add mushrooms, 1/4 cup of the chicken stock and paprika. Blend well and cook for 6-8 mins.
3. Pour in remaining stock and cook a further 3 mins.
4. Return beef and any residual juices to pan with mushrooms, reduce heat to low and stir gently. Pour in sour cream, heat through, garnish with dill and serve with hot buttered noodles, or rice or mashed potatoes. Serves 4.

Variation: cheaper cuts of beef can be used, in which case it would be wise to marinate these before frying. A longer cooking time also may be necessary in step 1 above.

BLACK PUDDING

A perfect "one pot wonder" that will satisfy any hoarde of complaining flatmates when it is your turn to cook.

in the

This is the ideal opportunity to impress with a dish that looks a lot more difficult than it is. The cooking time is invariably longer than the preparation and the aroma of cooking food is a welcome sensation for anyone returning home for the evening.

oven

HAM AND POTATO BAKE

1 cup grated cheddar cheese
3/4 cup cottage cheese
1/4 cup grated parmesan cheese
1/4 cup sliced spring onions
3/4 cup sour cream
Freshly ground black pepper
2 large potatoes, cooked and cubed (about 2 cups)
1 cup small broccoli florets, lightly cooked
1 cup diced cooked ham

1. Preheat oven to 180°C. Grease a 1.5 litre casserole.
2. In large bowl gently mix together 1/2 cup of cheddar, all the other cheeses, spring onions and sour cream. Add a grinding of black pepper.
3. Add vegetables and ham to the cheese mixture and stir until thoroughly coated. Spoon mixture into prepared casserole, smooth the top and sprinkle over remaining grated cheese.
4. Cover casserole tightly with foil and bake at 180°C for 20 mins.
5. Uncover and bake further 10 mins until golden brown. Serve immediately. Serves 3-4 (with salad).

ITALIAN TOMATO AND TUNA RICE PILAF

2 T olive oil
1 finely chopped onion
2 t **MASTERFOODS** freshly crushed garlic
1 1/2 cups **UNCLE BEN'S** long grain rice
1 x 370g jar **DOLMIO** traditional tomato sauce
1 1/2 cups water
1 x 185g can tuna, drained well
Salt and pepper to taste
80g tasty cheese, finely grated
1/4 cup chopped Italian parsley

1. Heat oil in a heavy-based pan.
2. Add onion and garlic and cook until onion is softened.
3. Cook UNCLE BEN'S rice to packet directions.
4. Mix rice and onions.
5. Stir in DOLMIO tomato sauce and water.
6. Place rice mixture in ovenproof dish and cover with lid. Cook in a preheated oven at 180°C for 15 mins until all liquid has been absorbed by the rice.
7. Remove from the oven, stir in tuna and season to taste.
8. Sprinkle the grated cheese and parsley on top. Serves 4.

MACARONI BAKE

1 x 365g jar **DOLMIO** sauce for carbonara
250g spinach
2 cups macaroni, cooked and drained
400–500g minced beef, cooked and drained
Freshly ground black pepper to taste
1 cup grated tasty cheese

1. Combine sauce for carbonara, spinach, macaroni, beef and pepper in a bowl.
2. Spoon into a heatproof, buttered dish and sprinkle with cheese.
3. Bake at 180°C for 1/2 hour to 3/4 hour or until brown and bubbling.
4. Serve with crusty French bread.

Variations: omit beef and use minced lamb, chicken or seafood.

OVEN-BAKED SALSA CHICKEN

1 kilo chicken pieces, wings and legs
1 T olive oil
1 T lemon juice
2 T **MASTERFOODS** parsley flakes
1/2 cup **MASTERFOODS** hot chunky salsa

1. Preheat oven to 180°C.
2. Combine chicken with all other ingredients in a baking dish.
3. Place in oven and allow to cook for 35–40 mins until chicken is cooked through. Serves 4.

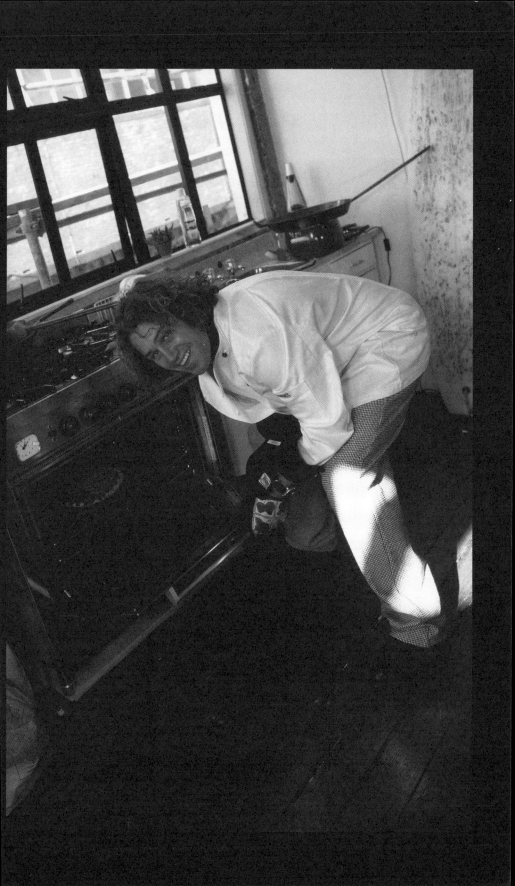

ONE-POT CHICKEN

3 medium potatoes, thinly sliced
2 carrots, thinly sliced
1 stick celery, thinly sliced
1 medium sized chicken
1 x 365g jar **DOLMIO** sauce for carbonara
1/3 cup chopped parsley or coriander

1. Place vegetables in base of a medium casserole dish.
2. Sit chicken on top, breast side down, and pour over carbonara sauce.
3. Cover and slowly braise at 180°C for 2 hours or until cooked and tender, turning chicken after one hour.
4. Lift chicken onto serving dish and keep hot.
5. Purée sauce, vegetables and parsley in a food processor, reheat and serve with chicken.
6. Any leftovers can be served as an excellent soup.

Variations: Use chicken portions instead of whole chicken. Add chopped bacon/and or mushrooms.

MOUSSAKA

3 small eggplants
Salt
6 T olive oil
Flour
1 onion, chopped
1 clove garlic, crushed
1 T oil
400g diced boneless lamb
1 1/2 cups **DOLMIO** traditional tomato sauce
2 eggs
2 T flour
750g plain yoghurt
4 T grated parmesan cheese
Salt and freshly ground black pepper

1. Cut unpeeled eggplant into longways slices 5 mm thick. Sprinkle with salt and leave for 1 hour.
2. Heat 6 T oil in heavy-based frying pan. Dry eggplant, dust with flour, then fry slices for 3-4 mins each side or until golden. Set aside to drain on kitchen paper.
3. Make meat sauce by heating oil in same pan and cooking chopped onion and garlic in this until tender (3-4 mins).
4. Add diced lamb and brown well.
5. Pour in DOLMIO tomato sauce, cover and simmer gently for about 20 mins.
6. Heat oven to 180°C and grease deep ovenproof dish.
7. Make sauce by heating 2 eggs until frothy, blending in flour, then whisking in yoghurt and half the parmesan cheese.
8. To assemble, layer eggplant slices and meat sauce in dish, ending with vegetable layer. Pour over white sauce, sprinkle with remaining parmesan and seasonings. Bake at 180°C for 1 hour or until golden brown and set. Serves 4-5.

LASAGNE

2 T olive oil
1 t MASTERFOODS crushed garlic
500g lean mince
1 x 575g jar DOLMIO traditional tomato and basil sauce
1 bunch silverbeet, shredded
500g cottage cheese
1 egg
2 sheets fresh lasagne
50g shredded parmesan
1 T MASTERFOODS oregano leaves

1. Sauté garlic and mince in oil, until mince is browned.
2. Add DOLMIO and simmer for 1/2 hour.
3. Blanch silverbeet until wilted and mix together with cottage cheese and egg.
4. In lasagne dish layer meat sauce, pasta sheet, silverbeet and cheese.
5. Sprinkle with parmesan and oregano.
6. Bake for 30 mins at 180°C. Serves 8.

SLOPPY JOES

10 large potatoes
1/4 cup chicken stock
1 T MASTERFOODS crushed garlic
2 sticks celery, chopped
500g minced beef
1 x 425g can MASTERFOODS red kidney beans
3/4 cup DOLMIO traditional tomato sauce
1/2 T MASTERFOODS mixed herbs
2 T MASTERFOODS parsley flakes

1. Scrub potatoes. Bake at 200°C for an hour.
2. Heat stock, add MASTERFOODS crushed garlic and celery. Cook, stirring over heat, for 1 min.
3. Add mince, stirring until well browned. Cover and cook gently for about 10 mins or until mince is tender.
4. Stir in MASTERFOODS red kidney beans, DOLMIO sauce and bring to the boil. Simmer covered for 3 mins.
5. Stir in mixed herbs and parsley flakes.
6. Splice tip of each potato in a cross. Force potato open to expose flesh. Spoon filling in the centre. Serves 5.

CREAMY FISH PIES

500g boneless white fish
1 T butter
1 T olive oil
1 x 365g jar DOLMIO sauce for carbonara
1 T chopped dill, optional
3-4 medium potatoes, cooked
extra butter and milk
1 cup parmesan cheese
extra dill, slices lemon for garnish

1. Steam, microwave or stirfry strips of fresh fish in butter and oil until just cooked.
2. Stir in sauce for carbonara and dill.
3. Gently heat through. Spoon into 4 ovenproof dishes
4. Mash potatoes, adding milk and butter.
5. Spoon over fish, sprinkle with cheese and bake at 180°C for 30 mins or until brown and bubbling.
6. Serve garnished with lemon slices and chopped dill. Serves 4.

MUM'S SHEPHERD'S PIE

1 onion, finely chopped
4 T butter
1 kg cooked roast lamb (or roast beef), minced
1 T Worcester sauce
1 t salt
1/4 t pepper
2 c green beans, cooked
1 cup packet-mix brown gravy
6 cups mashed potatoes
1 cup grated cheese

1. Preheat oven to 180°C. Grease a large baking dish.
2. Sauté onion in butter. Add minced cooked meat and combine well, then stir through Worcester sauce, seasonings, green beans well drained and cup of brown gravy.
3. Spoon mixture into baking dish and smooth over top. Spread over the mashed potatoes, fluffing up with a fork and making sure no meat is visible.
4. Sprinkle over the grated cheese and bake for approx. 30 mins until pie is well heated and topping golden and crisp. Serves 6.

PiZZA

2 large bought pizza bases (or make your
    own – see opposite)
1 cup **DOLMiO** traditional tomato sauce
1 t **MASTERFOODS** italian herbs
4 pinches **MASTERFOODS** garlic powder
Freshly ground black pepper
Toppings of your choice (see opposite)
200g mozzarella cheese
Olives or anchovies for garnish

1. Spread each base with 1/2 cup DOLMIO sauce.
2. Season with Italian herbs, garlic powder and pepper.
3. Arrange your favourite toppings on this base (see
   over for some popular combos).
4. Cover each topped pizza with 100g mozzarella and
   dot with halved pitted olives or anchovy slices.
5. Bake at 200°C for 15 min. Serve hot.

EASY PIZZA BASE

If there are no readymade bases left in the freezer, this scone-type dough is easy and tastes just as good. The following should make enough dough for 2 medium-large bases, depending on the thickness you prefer.

> 2 cups flour
> 2 t baking powder
> 1 T oil
> 1/2 cup milk (or more)
> 75g grated cheese
> 1/4 t salt

1. Sift flour and baking powder into a bowl.
2. Whisk together oil and milk in a cup.
3. Add grated cheese and salt to flour and fork through, then slowly pour in oil/milk mixture and blend to make a soft but not wet dough.
4. With floured hands, divide dough ball in two, then roll each piece into a rough circle.
5. Lightly oil two pizza tins and push the dough into each tin so that it covers the whole surface thinly.
6. Top each pizza as outlined in the recipe opposite. Bake at 230°C for 10-15 min.

SAVOURY PIZZA COMBOS

Arrange the following over pizza base: spread with herbed Italian style (basil/garlic) tomato sauce. Top with grated colby or mozzarella cheese.

Ham/pineapple/onion rings/olives;
ham or bacon strips/mushrooms/tomato slices;
baked beans/bacon/onion rings;
chicken/capsicum and tomato slices/olives;
chicken/pineapple/avocado/spring onions;
salami/tomato slices/olives;
tuna or salmon or any uncooked shellfish/tomato and capsicum slices/onion rings/olives.

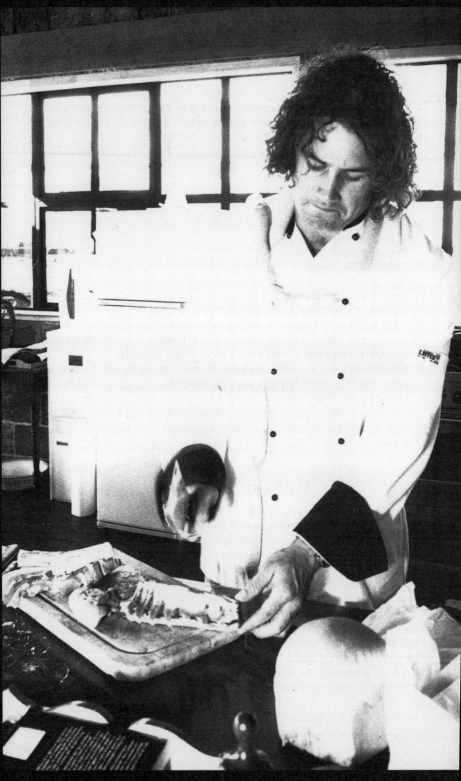

BOBOTIE

2 T oil	2 T lemon juice
1 onion, sliced	1 T sugar
1 T MASTERFOODS	1/4 cup raisins
madras curry powder	1/4 cup sliced almonds
1 apple, peeled, cored	4 bayleaves
and chopped	1 egg
500g beef mince	1 cup milk
2 slices bread	Salt and pepper
1/2 cup beef stock or water	

1. Preheat oven to 150°C.
2. In large heavy-based casserole dish heat the oil.
3. Fry together onion, curry powder and apple, then add mince and cook until colour has just gone from meat.
4. Soak bread in stock, then stir into the mixture with the lemon juice, sugar, raisins and almonds. Mix well and remove from heat.
5. Flatten top, then lay over the bayleaves.
6. Beat together egg and milk and season well. Pour over the meat mixture.
7. Bake at 150°C for 1 hour or until custard has set. Serves 4-6.

BBQ SPARE RIBS

1 kilo beef spare ribs
1 t honey
2 T olive oil
2 T light soy sauce
1/2 cup MASTERFOODS hot chunky salsa
1 t MASTERFOODS garlic granules

1. Preheat oven to 180°C.
2. Combine ribs with all remaining ingredients and allow to marinate in a stainless steel baking dish for 30 mins.
3. Place in oven and bake for 1 hour until ribs are crisp and tender. Serves 4.

ROAST DINNERS

For 4-6 people a roast meat dinner is still a most economical meal. There are countless dishes you can make with roast meat leftovers, and plain cold sliced roast meat is great for sandwiches.

Roasting meat is a simple process, but the following hints will ensure a hassle-free meal.

Whatever sized roast you buy, be it beef, lamb, pork or poultry, make sure you have an adequately sized roasting dish for it. This allows all-round heat circulation and definitely improves the quality of your roast. Alternatively, you can put the joint directly on the rungs of your oven shelf, with the roasting dish underneath. This way you can fit lots more veges in the roasting dish and the joint will cook more quickly and evenly. Oven bags are good value, helping to cook the meat evenly and more quickly.

Have your roast at room temperature for at least an hour before you pop it into the oven, and always put the joint in fat side uppermost. Unless the meat is very lean, or you've flung together a flavoursome marinade you don't want to waste, it should not need basting (venison excepted). Never add the dripping of one type of animal to the joint of another, i.e. pork dripping for a beef roast.

If you have a friendly butcher, it is a good idea to request him or her to take the bone out of your lamb leg, for example. There will be a good cavity for stuffing if you wish, the leg will cook more quickly and also be easier to carve.

Cooking times vary greatly for roasts, depending on your oven's efficiency, the weight/size of the joint, its age and how it has been prepared. The following chart will give you a general idea of how long you should allow, but if you are following a special recipe, always be guided by that, for every method is different.

ROASTING TIMES FOR MEAT

	Oven Temp	Time per kg of meat
Chicken extra*	180°C	60 mins + 10–20 mins
Pork	180°C	70 mins
Lamb	180°C	70 mins medium
		90 mins well done
Beef	160°–180°C	30 mins rare
		45 mins medium
		50 mins well done

*Chicken must not be undercooked. It's done when the legs can be easily separated from the body, or only clear juices are released when skewered in the thickest part. If juices are still pink, return to oven for further 5–10 mins.

BASIC MEAT GRAVY

1 T flour or cornflour
1/4 cup water
Salt and pepper
More water, or wine, or water in which vegetables
   have been cooked

1. Combine flour and water in a cup until lumpfree and creamy.
2. On a low heat put roasting dish containing pan juices and any shreds of meat remaining from chicken, pork, lamb or beef roast. Stir and scrape to loosen scraps.
3. Add 1/2 – 1 cup liquid, stirring well, and bring to boil.
4. Add flour/water mixture and keep stirring while gently boiling. As mixture thickens, add more water or the wine. Season and serve with roasted meat on the plate, with remainder in a hot jug at table.

SiMPLE STUFFED CHOOK

1 fresh chicken, about 1.5 kg
2 T butter
1/2 cup finely chopped onion
2 rashers bacon, rind removed and chopped
1/2 stalk celery, chopped
1 t MASTERFOODS mixed herbs
1 T fresh parsley, finely chopped
Salt and freshly ground black pepper
2 slices fresh bread, crumbled
3 T rolled oats
2 T water
1 egg
1 T cooking oil

1. Preheat oven to 180°C.
2. Prepare the stuffing by melting butter in frying pan and gently cooking onion, celery and bacon together.
3. Remove from heat and add dried herbs. Add chopped parsley, pepper and salt, then put aside to cool.
4. Add breadcrumbs, oats and water to stuffing. Beat egg and stir in, mixing well.
5. Rinse and dry chicken, making sure you remove giblets/heart etc. if they are inside the bird.
6. Push stuffing into the cavity of the chicken. Truss bird into a compact shape with string.
7. Put chicken on a rack in baking dish, dribble over oil and roast at 180°C for 70-80 mins, checking after 60 mins.
8. Transfer roast to heated plate and keep hot. Drain off fat from roasting dish and make gravy as on p. 69. Serves 4-6.

HERBED LEG OF LAMB

1 leg lamb, 2-3 kg (at room temp. for at least 1
   hour)
1/4 t MASTERFOODS rosemary leaves
2 cloves garlic, cut in slivers
Salt and pepper
Flour
Lamb dripping, or 4 t any cooking oil

1. Heat oven to 180°C.
2. Dry meat with paper towel. Make cuts in meat near
   bone and insert garlic slivers and one or two
   rosemary sprigs.
3. Rub joint well with salt and pepper, then dust with
   flour.
4. Put meat on rack in roasting dish, dab with dripping
   pieces or oil, then scatter over remaining rosemary.
5. Roast until done (see chart on p. 69), then remove
   meat to heated carving dish and pour off all the fat
   except last 3 T approx.
6. Make gravy in roasting pan as described on p. 69
   and serve this over the meat slices.

Variations: Other herbs, fresh or dried, can be used,
especially mint, sage and thyme.

The leg can be boned and the cavity filled with herbed
stuffing, made as for chicken roast opposite, or any
other stuffing you fancy. (Cooked herbed or spiced rice
is good, or a mixture of dried chopped fruits and 1 t
curry powder substituted for the herbs in the chicken
stuffing recipe.)

Root vegetables and other suitable types such as
onions, capsicum and squash, can be roasted in the
oven with your joint. Have these all cut to similar size
and dredged with seasoned flour. Add after roast has
been in oven 45 mins. Turn veges occasionally to
prevent sticking. After 45 mins or so, check for
tenderness with a fork. Once veges are cooked,
remove to serving dish and keep hot till needed.

Sizzlers

Every kiwi bloke worth his salt, considers himself unparalleled in his ability over a BBQ or grill. It is truly a very social scene when a barbie is ignited and you have a couple of

beers and good company. Often, given this atmosphere, a mistake in the preparation of the food will be overlooked by those present. The perfect forum in which to display and voice one's talent.

DEVILLED KIDNEYS

lamb kidneys diced thick (6–8)
2t butter
2t grated onion
1t salt
1/4t salt
1/4t MASTERFOODS Madras curry
dash worcester sauce
chopped parsley

Fry grated onion and lamb kidneys in butter. Add seasonings. Serve on buttered toast.

LIVER AND BACON

600g liver
8 rashers bacon
flour for coating
chopped parsley

Skin liver. Cut into 1/2 inch strips. Coat in flour gently. Cook with bacon. Remove from pan and use meat drippings with water to make gravy. Add some chopped parsley. Serve with mashed potato. Serves 4.

SAUSAGE BREW

1 can beer
2 T oil
2 cloves garlic
2 T soy sauce
2 t **MASTERFOODS** wholegrain mustard
1 T tomato or barbecue sauce
1 t brown sugar
Freshly ground black pepper
1 onion, peeled and sliced
2 t cornflour
1 T vinegar

1. Combine beer, 1 T oil, 1 garlic clove, soy sauce,
   mustard, tomato sauce, sugar and pepper in a deep
   dish and stir well.
2. Prick the sausages all over and put in the marinade
   for an hour or so.
3. Heat 1 T oil in a large heavy frying pan. Drain
   sausages, reserving marinade. Cook sausages over
   medium heat until well browned on all sides. Remove
   from pan and drain off any fat.
4. Cook until tender the sliced onion and garlic clove.
   Add the marinade to the pan and bring to a slow boil,
   stirring constantly. Return the sausages, cover and
   simmer for 15 mins or until the sausages are cooked.
5. Combine cornflour and vinegar and add to pan. Bring
   to the boil and stir until liquid thickens.
6. Serve sausages and gravy hot with rice or potatoes.
   Serves 4.

CHICKEN SATAY WITH PEANUT SAUCE

500g chicken thigh or breast fillets
1 onion, roughly chopped
2 t fresh ginger, finely chopped
2 T lemon juice
1 T soy sauce
1 T sesame oil
1 T brown sugar
1 x 360g jar KAN TONG Malaysian satay sauce,
heated
2 x UNCLE BEN'S Boil-in-Bag sachets

1. Cut the chicken meat into small cubes and put into marinade of next 4 ingredients, made as follows, for 1 hour or more.
2. In a food processor blend to a smooth purée the onions, ginger, lemon juice and soy sauce.
3. Pour purée into a bowl, add sesame oil and stir in sugar until dissolved. Add chicken pieces and put aside for at least 1 hour, or overnight in fridge.
4. While chicken is marinating, prepare bamboo satay skewers by soaking in cold water for at least 15 mins.
5. Thread about 6 pieces of chicken on to pointed end of each skewer. (Leave rest of skewer bare but don't push meat bits too close as they will cook better with space between.)
6. Barbecue or grill satays over/under moderate heat, turning skewers so the chicken pieces cook evenly. They should need only 3-4 mins to cook through.
7. Serve on hot rice with warm peanut sauce poured over. Serves 3-4.

RISSOLES

3 slices white bread, chopped
1/4 cup water
500g minced beef, pork, veal or uncooked chicken
1 onion, finely chopped
2 cloves garlic, crushed
Salt and freshly ground black pepper
1 T MASTERFOODS italian herbs
2 T chopped fresh parsley
1 egg, beaten
dry breadcrumbs
oil for frying

1. Put bread slices in bowl, add water and soak for 2 mins then drain, squeezing out all excess water.
2. Combine bread, meat, onion, garlic, seasonings, dried herbs, parsley and beaten egg in bowl.
3. Shape mixture into rissoles, toss in breadcrumbs and shake off excess.
4. Heat oil in heavy pan, add rissoles and fry over medium heat for about 5 mins or until well browned all over and cooked through. Drain on kitchen paper.
5. Serve rissoles with brown gravy or a tangy sauce. Serves 4.

BARBECUED STEAK

6 Scotch fillet or rib eye steaks, about 2.5 cm thick
1/2 cup soy sauce
2 cloves garlic, 1 crushed and 1 just halved
1 t finely chopped fresh ginger
1/4 cup sesame seeds
1/4 cup peanut or vegetable oil
1/4 cup red wine
Freshly ground black pepper

1. Put steak in shallow glass dish. Rub over with halved clove of garlic.
2. Combine in a bowl the soy sauce, crushed garlic, ginger, sesame seeds, oil, wine and pepper. Pour this marinade over the steak, cover with cling wrap and let stand 30 mins.
4. Drain steaks, reserving marinade, and pat dry the meat with paper towel.
5. Barbecue steaks on greased grill over glowing coals for about 7 mins each side, brushing with marinade and turning a couple of times. Serves 6.

SPANISH CHICKEN

1/2 cup soy sauce
1/2 cup dry sherry
1/2 cup cold water
Salt and pepper
1.5kg chicken pieces
Flour
Pinch MASTERFOODS ground cumin seed
60g butter
2 cloves garlic, crushed
2 cups water
1 large onion, peeled and sliced
1 capsicum, green or red, sliced
60g stuffed green olives, halved
Hot rice for 5

1. Combine soy sauce, sherry, water and seasonings in a bowl.
2. Marinate chicken pieces in soy-sherry mixture for 3-4 hours.
3. Drain chicken. Reserve marinade.
4. Put about 3/4 cup flour in plastic bag with cumin powder, close top and shake to mix. Coat chicken pieces in flour in the bag. Shake off excess.
5. In a heavy-based casserole melt butter. Sauté chicken pieces in this until golden brown.
6. Add crushed garlic, the remaining marinade and the water. Simmer, covered, for 30 min.
7. Add onion, capsicum, and olives and simmer 10 mins more, uncovered, or until chicken is tender. Serve with hot rice. Serves 4-5.

PORK SCHNITZELS WITH SOUR CREAM

1 large bunch of silverbeet or spinach
Salt and pepper
1 T oil
1 T butter
6 pork schnitzels
1 carton (400g approx) sour cream
Pinch MASTERFOODS ground nutmeg

1. Wash and roughly chop silverbeet or spinach, then cook 2-3 mins in boiling salted water. Drain vegetable well, stir in seasonings then spread over bottom of serving dish. Keep warm.
2. Heat butter and oil in heavy-based pan. Fry schnitzels in this, approx. 3 mins each side.
3. Lay cooked schnitzels on the greens. Pour over the sour cream and sprinkle with nutmeg. Serves 3.

HAM STEAKS WAIKIKI

4 ham steaks
1 x 450g can pineapple rings and juice
1 T oil
1 T vinegar
1 T MASTERFOODS wholegrain mustard
1 spring onion, sliced finely
1/2 sweet red pepper, finely diced
Salt and pepper
1 T butter

1. Make a marinade by combining pineapple juice with enough cold water to make 1 cup. In a flat dish mix this with oil, vinegar, mustard, spring onion, red pepper and seasonings.
2. Trim any fat and the rind from ham steaks. Make small cut at regular intervals all round the edges of steaks, to prevent curling when fried. Lay the meat in the marinade for 10 mins.
3. Drain the meat, retaining all the marinade.
4. Melt the butter in frying pan and fry the steaks quickly in this, making sure the meat is heated through and nicely browned. Transfer to heated plate and keep hot.
5. Scrape down any juices, which may be caramelised, from the pan, then add marinade and pineapple rings and simmer gently over low heat until fruit is hot and marinade reduced.
6. Arrange hot pineapple rings on top of each steak, spoon over sauce from the pan and serve at once. Serves 4.

BLACK PUDDING

A proper little sizzler – great on the barbie with a bit of beer drizzled over.

Veges on

To be perfectly honest i've never been big on veges unless with a roast. However, i feel it is necessary to be culturally sensitive and humour the greenies out there who insist that veges are the cornerstone of nutrition. Everything in moderation is my advice.

the Table

PUMPKIN SOUP

1 kg fresh pumpkin
1 large onion, chopped
3 rashers bacon
2 T butter
1 t MASTERFOODS ground coriander
1 t MASTERFOODS ground cumin
Salt and black pepper
10 cups chicken or vegetable stock
Fresh parsley to garnish

1. Peel pumpkin, remove seeds, hollow out inside and cut into chunks.
2. In a large saucepan lightly fry the onion and bacon in butter for 5 mins.
3. Add the pumpkin, coriander, cumin, salt and pepper. Mix well, cover and cook for about 10 mins.
4. Add the chicken stock and simmer for 45 mins.
5. Purée or mash to ensure soup is smooth
6. Garnish with chopped parsley. Serves 6.

GOLDEN KUMARA SOUP

50g butter
2 large onions, diced
1 large carrot, shredded
5 cups chicken stock
1 cup orange juice
750g kumara, pref. golden variety, peeled and cubed
Salt and pepper to taste
Orange rind, finely shredded, for garnish
Chopped parsley

1. In large heavy-based pan melt butter. Add onions and carrot and cook over low heat until tender.
2. Add stock, orange juice and kumara. Bring to the boil, cover and simmer on low heat for 20-30 mins.
3. Cool soup slightly then purée or sieve mixture.
4. Return soup to pan, add seasonings and serve when it is hot but not boiling. Garnish with orange rind and chopped parsley. Serves 6.

GAZPACHO

Chilled Fresh Tomato Soup

3/4 cup chopped mint leaves
1 onion, diced
2 cucumbers, peeled and roughly chopped
1 clove garlic, crushed
1 x 425g can tomato purée
2 T lemon juice
3 T olive oil
1/2 t salt
pinch cayenne pepper
3 large tomatoes, seeded, skinned and chopped
1 capsicum, seeded and chopped
750 ml carton plain yoghurt
2 T finely chopped mint for garnish

1. Put all ingredients except yoghurt and mint garnish into a food processor and blend until smooth.
2. Pour into large jug, cover and chill for 4 hours or overnight.
3. Stir 600 ml of the yoghurt through the chilled soup and pour into individual bowls.
4. Swirl 1 T of yoghurt on top of each serve and sprinkle with chopped mint. Accompany with French bread, fried croutons or nacho chips. Serves 4-6.

KUMARA PIE

3 eggs
1 T olive oil
1/2 cup cottage cheese
1 orange, juice and zest
1/2 T MASTERFOODS lemon pepper
5 medium kumara, peeled and grated
1 onion, chopped
1/2 T MASTERFOODS crushed garlic
1 cup self-raising wholemeal flour
1/2 cup MASTERFOODS bacon-flavoured chips
Grated cheese

1. Beat together eggs, oil, cottage cheese, orange juice and zest, lemon pepper.
2. Combine with kumara, onion, garlic, flour and bacon chips. Retain some chips for topping.
3. Pile into greased flan dish, sprinkle with grated cheese and bacon chips.
4. Bake at 190°C for 40-45 mins until golden brown.

ITALIAN SPICED POTATOES

750g baby new potatoes, washed and dried
1/3 cup olive oil
2 t MASTERFOODS freshly crushed garlic
1 t MASTERFOODS italian herbs
1/2 t MASTERFOODS ground chillies

1. Cut potatoes into large chunks. Heat oil in a baking dish with freshly crushed garlic in a hot oven (200°C) for 2-3 mins.
2. Add potatoes. Stir well to coat with oil and garlic. Sprinkle with Italian herbs and ground chillies.
3. Return to moderate oven (180-190°C) for 1 hour, turning potatoes every 15 mins until golden and crisp.

ZUCCHINI FRITATA

600g zucchini, sliced
2 T olive oil
60g bacon strips, grilled crisp and brown
Salt and freshly ground pepper
6 large eggs, well beaten
1 T grated parmesan

1. Sauté zucchini with oil in heavy frying pan until soft. Remove to a large bowl. (Reserve oil from pan.)
2. To the bowl add bacon, seasonings, eggs and cheese. Gently stir to combine.
3. Wipe out frying pan with kitchen paper. Return the reserved olive oil and reheat.
4. Pour egg mixture into heated pan and cook on one side, pulling in the edges a little to allow uncooked mixture to run underneath.
5. When only a little of the mixture on top remains uncooked place a warmed flat plate over the pan and invert the fritata. Help to turn it out with a metal spatula – and a little patience.
6. Slide inverted fritata back into hot pan to cook top, but take off heat while the centre is still soft.
7. Slide on to hot plate and slice into wedges to serve. Serves 4-6 with salad.

HINT: If you have a grill, cook the top side of the fritata under this until golden brown, instead of inverting it as in step 5.

Variations: Many other vegetables can be used successfully in fritata: cauliflower, artichokes, broccoli, asparagus, eggplant, kumara, potatoes, capsicum and tomatoes are all very tasty cooked by this method.

VEGETABLE CURRY

2 t curry powder, or to taste
1 t **MASTERFOODS** ground cumin seed
2 T butter, melted
2 onions, sliced
2 cloves garlic, crushed
4 medium potatoes, peeled and sliced
400g pumpkin, peeled, deseeded and chunked
2 sticks celery, sliced
1/2 red pepper, finely chopped
1/2 green pepper, finely chopped
Salt and pepper
2 t lemon juice
1/2 cup vegetable stock

1. Stir curry powder and cumin seeds into melted butter in heavy casserole dish.
2. Add onions and garlic and sauté till tender (4 mins).
3. Add rest of vegetables to pan. Stir in seasonings, lemon juice and stock. Cover and simmer vegetables until just tender. Cook uncovered few mins more until any liquid is absorbed. Serve hot or cold. Serves 4.

VEGETABLES AU GRATIN

1 x 365g jar **DOLMIO** sauce for carbonara
24 spears fresh asparagus
1 1/2 cups each small florets cauliflower and
    broccoli
thinly sliced carrot
any frozen or canned vegetables
Mushroom
1 cup grated cheese

1. Gently heat sauce for carbonara until boiling.
2. Steam or microwave vegetables until just tender.
3. Drain well.
4. Transfer to a shallow oven-proof dish.
5. Cover with sauce, sprinkle with cheese and brown under the grill or in a oven at 200°C for about 20 mins. Serves 4.

RATATOUiLLE
Mediterranean Vegetable Stew

8 T best quality olive oil
2 onions, sliced
2 capsicum, seeded and sliced
2 eggplant, cubed
2 zucchini, cut in 15 mm slices
4-6 ripe tomatoes, skinned, seeded and chopped
Salt and freshly ground black pepper
1 T chopped parsley
1 T chopped basil
Pinch MASTERFOODS oregano
2 cloves garlic, crushed

1. Gently heat olive oil in large heavy-based pan.
2. Add onion slices and cook until transparent.
3. Add capsicum and eggplant, and 4 mins later, zucchini and tomatoes.
4. The vegetables should not be fried but just stewed in the oil, so cover pan and simmer gently for 30 mins.
5. Add seasonings and herbs, including crushed garlic, and cook gently, uncovered, for further 10-15 mins until ratatouille is well mixed.
6. Serve hot from the casserole, with lots of crusty fresh bread. Can also be served cold as an entrée. Serves 4 as a meal.

HERB 'N' MUSTARD COBS

125g butter
1-2t MASTERFOODS freshly crushed garlic
1/3 cup MASTERFOODS herb mustard
1 T parmesan cheese, freshly grated
MASTERFOODS ground black pepper, to taste
4-6 sweetcorn cobs

1. Cream butter and beat in garlic, mustard, cheese and pepper.
2. Use to coat cobs and place in a shallow dish in a single layer.
3. Cover and microwave on high for 4 mins or until cooked.
4. Cut each cob into 3 or 4 pieces and serve with melted butter mixture on top.

STUFFED GREEN AND RED PEPPERS

20 black olives, pitted
4 slices salami, skinned
6 medium peppers, green, red or any other colour
    available at season's height
1 cup olive oil
1 cup breadcrumbs
30g toasted pinenuts
2 T sultanas
2 T chopped parsley
Salt and freshly ground black pepper
12 slices gruyere cheese

1. Preheat oven to 180°C.
2. Chop the olives and salami and in a large bowl mix with all the ingredients except peppers and cheese.
3. Slice peppers in half lengthwise and scoop out seeds and thick pith.
4. In each pepper place a good spoonful of the stuffing. Pile as high as possible.
5. Cover with gruyere slices and put in baking dish. Add enough oil to ensure peppers will not stick and bake for 30 mins at 180°C, until cheese is melted and stuffing well heated. Serves 4 as light meal, or use on antipasto platter.

TANGY BEAN SALAD

1 x 425g can
MASTERFOODS three bean
  mix
125g green beans
1/4 head cauliflower
1 orange, segmented

DRESSING
1/2 cup oil
4 T white wine vinegar

1/4 t MASTERFOODS all
  purpose seasoning
2 T orange juice
Pinch MASTERFOODS
  garlic powder
1/4 t MASTERFOODS
  sweet basil leaves
1/4 t MASTERFOODS hot
  English mustard
1 T MASTERFOODS
  chives

1. Drain the can of three bean mix.
2. Blanch the green beans and cauliflower in boiling water.
3. Refresh quickly under running cold water.
4. Combine the dressing ingredients in a jar and shake vigorously.
5. Pour over salad and allow to stand for 30 mins.
6. Decorate with orange segments before serving.

CRUNCHY BANANA SALAD

2 t MASTERFOODS
  Madras curry powder
2 t oil
1 small onion, diced
5 firm medium bananas
6 radishes, cubed

2 stalks celery, diced
1/2 cup bean sprouts
Salt and pepper
1/4 cup lemon juice
1/2 t dry mustard
Lettuce leaves

1. Combine curry powder and oil and heat gently for 1 min. Set aside for flavours to blend.
2. Crisp diced onion in iced water for 10 min. Drain.
3. Peel and slice bananas into a bowl.
4. Add celery, radishes, onion and bean sprouts. Season.
5. Combine cooled curry mixture, lemon juice and mustard until smooth and pour over the salad. Toss lightly to blend.
6. Arrange lettuce leaves on flat dish and top with banana salad. Serves 4-6.

NOUVEAU SALAD NICOISE

500g baby new potatoes, cooked and halved
1 x 425g can **MASTERFOODS** red kidney beans
1 cup corn kernels
2 salmon fillets
Juice 1/2 lemon
1 punnet cherry tomatoes
1 x 170g jar artichokes, drained
125g black olives, pitted
125g feta cheese, cubed
4 hard-boiled eggs, quartered
1 x 45g can anchovy fillets, drained

DRESSING
1/2 cup olive oil
2 T **MASTERFOODS** sweet basil leaves
1 t **MASTERFOODS** Dijon mustard
1/2 t **MASTERFOODS** freshly crushed garlic

1. Combine potatoes, beans and corn. Set aside.
2. Place salmon on a foil-lined grill tray. Drizzle with lemon juice. Grill for 2-3 mins or until flesh flakes easily when tested with fork.
3. Flake salmon and set aside.
4. Combine tomatoes, artichokes, olives and feta. Set aside.
5. Arrange salad ingredients and flaked salmon in groups on a serving platter. Top with eggs and anchovies.
6. To prepare dressing, whisk together all ingredients. Drizzle generously over the salad. Serve with crusty bread. Serves 3-4.

POTATO SALAD

9 small potatoes (about 750g), washed and peeled
1 cup natural yoghurt
3/4 cup diced celery
1/2 cup thinly sliced spring onions
8 t red wine vinegar
4 t MASTERFOODS Dijon mustard
2 T chopped fresh dill
Freshly ground black pepper
Tomato quarters and dill sprigs for garnish

1. Put peeled potatoes in large pan with enough cold water to cover. Bring to boil over high heat, then reduce to medium, cover pan and cook potatoes until fork-tender (about 15 mins).
2. Drain potatoes in colander and leave until cool enough to handle. Cut warm potatoes into chunky pieces.
3. In a bowl combine potatoes, yoghurt, vegetables, vinegar, mustard, dill and pepper. Toss gently to combine and serve immediately, garnished with tomatoes and dill, or cover bowl with plastic wrap and refrigerate until needed. Serves 4-6.

GREEK SALAD

1 cucumber, peeled and sliced
1 large lettuce, washed and dried
1 bunch curly endive, washed and dried
2 tomatoes, cored and wedged
2 red or white onions, peeled, halved and then
    thinly sliced
1/2 cup olive oil
2 T white vinegar
2 cloves garlic, crushed
Salt and freshly ground black pepper
24 Greek black olives
125g feta cheese, cut in small cubes
6 anchovy fillets (optional)

1. In large salad bowl arrange cucumber slices.
2. Coarsely shred lettuce and endive with stainless steel knife and put on top of cucumber.
3. Heap onion slices in centre with tomato wedges.
4. Make a dressing by combining the oil, vinegar, garlic, salt and pepper. Sprinkle liberally over salad in the bowl.
6. Scatter black olives and feta cubes on top of salad and garnish with anchovies. Serve with lamb or veal dishes. Serves 4-6.

WALNUT AND APPLE COLESLAW

450g hard white cabbage, finely sliced
2 sticks celery, finely sliced
2 carrots, grated
2 apples, grated
1 1/2 t grated lemon rind
3 T lemon juice
4 T chopped walnuts
1/4 t carraway seeds
Salt and pepper
5 T mayonnaise
1 clove garlic
Few walnut halves, apple slices, watercress sprigs
    or parsley for garnish

1. In a bowl put all ingredients except mayonnaise, garlic and garnishes.
2. Add mayonnaise and mix gently through.
3. Cut in half the garlic clove and rub around a shallow serving dish.
4. Turn coleslaw into the dish and decorate with walnuts, apple slices and watercress or parsley. Keep cool until needed. Serves 4-6.

PESTO CROUTON SALAD

1/2 loaf French bread
1/2 jar DOLMIO PRIMA pesto sauce
    with roasted capsicum
Salad greens
1/4 cup vinaigrette
Parmesan cheese shavings

1. Cut bread into 1cm slices.
2. Grill bread until golden and crisp.
3. Spread with DOLMIO PRIMA pesto sauce and cut into cubes.
4. Prepare salad greens, washing and trimming.
5. Toss through croutons and vinaigrette.
6. Garnish with parmesan cheese and serve immediately. Serves 4.

LETTUCE CUPS

4 lettuce leaf 'cups'
2 cups alfalfa sprouts
1 cup mixed bean sprouts, e.g. snow pea, adzuki,
    mung bean, lentil or radish
1/4 cup plain unsweetened yoghurt
2 T mayonnaise
1 T finely chopped fresh mint
1 T finely chopped fresh parsley
1 spring onion, finely diced

1. Arrange washed and dried lettuce leaves on serving
   platter or individual plates.
2. Put 1/4 alfalfa sprouts in each lettuce cup, then top
   with 1/4 of the other sprouts.
3. Blend the yoghurt, mayonnaise, mint, parsley and
   spring onion to make a smooth dressing. Put a large
   spoonful of dressing on each lettuce cup. Serves 4.

HINT: This dressing is ideal with any other green leafy
salad and may also be used with cold potatoes.

BLACK PUDDING

If you get sick of those veges, then this is the one to
inspire your flagging appetite. Get the black pudding,
throw it in the frying pan and you'll be on your way to
an unparalleled feast.

All at

There is no doubt that seafood is amongst the best kai around.

Better still if caught by those indulging in the resulting meal. Many a struggling student has been revitalised in a trip to the local coastline to gather some food from the sea. Often this is best eaten on site on an open fire with a sheet of corrugated iron or tin billy to steam or boil the catch . . .

Sea

MUM'S CRAYFISH MAYONNAISE

1 egg
1 t salt
1 t cornflour
1/2 t mustard powder
1/4 t white pepper
2 Dsstpn sugar
1 cup cold milk
1/2 cup malt vinegar
1 t butter

1. Beat egg in a pot.
2. Add salt, cornflour, mustard powder, pepper and sugar. Mix.
3. Add cold milk and malt vinegar, stirring all the time. Heat until nearly boiling.
4. Remove from stove and add butter. Leave to stand.
5. Serve with crayfish.

ITALIAN SALSA MUSSELS

12 fresh mussels
2 t MASTERFOODS freshly crushed garlic
1 medium onion, finely chopped
1 T olive oil
1 jar of MASTERFOODS chunky medium salsa
Juice of 1 lemon
Grated parmesan cheese
1/2 cup finely chopped parsley

1. Scrub mussels in cold water.
2. Remove beards if possible.
3. Soak for 30 mins in cold water.
4. Boil large saucepan of water. Add mussels in their shells, cover pan tightly and cook quickly over heat for 5 mins. Mussels are ready when shells have opened.
5. Remove top half of shell. Set aside mussel in half shell.
6. In a frypan cook garlic and onion in oil over moderate heat until onions are tender. Add salsa and lemon juice.
7. Simmer for 5 mins, until hot.
8. Spoon salsa mixture over half mussels.
9. Top with parmesan cheese.
10. Place under grill for 3 mins to heat. Sprinkle with parsley and serve hot. Serves 2.

CAJUN FISH

1 red capsicum, seeded and peeled
1 tomato, peeled and chopped
1 onion, peeled and roughly chopped
1/2 cup olive oil
Juice 1 lime
2 t **MASTERFOODS** freshly crushed garlic
1 1/2 t **MASTERFOODS** cajun seasoning
1 1/2 t **MASTERFOODS** seasoned pepper
4 fish fillets

1. Process capsicum, tomato, onion, oil, lime juice, freshly crushed garlic, cajun seasoning and seasoned pepper in a food processor until a paste is formed.
2. Brush fish liberally with the paste. Allow to marinate for 30 mins.
3. Grill, BBQ or bake fish until flesh flakes easily when tested with a fork.
4. Serve with salad. Serves 4.

KINGFISH KEBABS

1kg kingfish or other firm-fleshed fish, cut into pieces
2 T olive oil
1/2 cup **MASTERFOODS** medium chunky salsa
Juice and rind of one lemon

1. Preheat grill or BBQ.
2. Coat fish with mixture of all other ingredients and then thread onto BBQ skewers.
3. Place on grill and cook for 3-4 mins on each side, turning once. Serves 4.

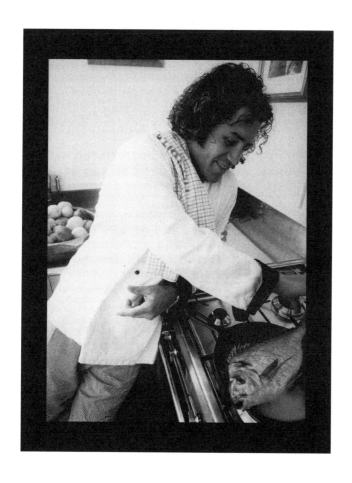

FISH PARCELS WITH GINGER LEMON MUSTARD SAUCE

4 boneless white fish fillets (600g approx.)
1 small onion, sliced
1 small lemon, sliced
1/2 cup lemon juice
Salt and pepper
Butter

1. Preheat oven to 180°C. Cut 4 squares of tinfoil (approx. 30 x 30 cm.)
2. Put a fish fillet in centre of each tinfoil square.
3. Arrange onion and lemon slices on top of fish. Sprinkle with lemon juice and seasoning. Add a dab of butter to each fillet.
4. Close parcels securely and place, joined side up, side by side on baking dish. Bake at 180°C for 15 mins or until flesh is just white. (Do not overcook.)
5. To serve, roll back tinfoil neatly around each fillet, retaining juices and lemon/onion slices. Spoon 2 T of the ginger lemon sauce on each fillet and pass jug with remaining sauce. Serves 4.

GINGER LEMON MUSTARD SAUCE

(Make ahead of fish preparation and warm through just before serving with above, or any other plain fish dish.)

1/4 cup fish stock
1/4 cup lemon juice
4 t MASTERFOODS
wholegrain mustard
1 T honey
3 t grated fresh ginger
2 T cornflour
2 T cold water
1/4 cup cream
Ground black pepper to taste

1. Combine first 5 ingredients in pan and bring to boil.
2. Reduce heat and simmer gently, uncovered, for 5 mins.
3. Blend cornflour and water. Stir into hot stock along with cream and pepper.
4. Cook over medium heat until sauce is thick, stirring all the time. Reserve while fish is being cooked. Serve warm in a heated jug.

SIMPLE SMOKED FISH SOUFFLE

2 T butter
3 T milk
1 cup cooked mashed potato
2 eggs, separated
1 x 310g tin smoked fish (or same amount of fresh
smoked fish)
2 T lemon juice
2 T chopped parsley

1. Preheat oven to 180°C. Grease 17 cm soufflé dish.
2. Warm together butter and milk in pan over low heat.
3. Beat mashed potatoes and egg yolks into butter and milk.
4. Add undrained fish, broken into small pieces, lemon juice and parsley.
5. In clean dry bowl beat the egg whites till stiff. Fold this into fish mixture.
6. Turn into greased soufflé dish and bake at 180°C for 45 mins or until soufflé is set firm. Serve immediately. Serves 4.

SOUTH SEA SALAD

750g very fresh snapper or tarakihi fillets
1 clove garlic, crushed
Juice of 4 lemons
1/4 cup tinned coconut cream
1 cucumber, peeled and cubed
1 onion, peeled and sliced thinly
3 spring onions, finely chopped, including green
   tops
2 hardboiled eggs, sliced
Parsley sprigs
MASTERFOODS ground paprika

1. Remove all skin and bones from fish and cut into small cubes.
2. Put into a glass or plastic bowl and add lemon juice.
3. Leave fish to marinate for at least 3 hours, preferably overnight. Turn fish occasionally, using a wooden spoon. (Avoid using any metal utensils or bowls for this recipe.)
4. Drain off lemon juice. Mix garlic with coconut cream and pour over fish. Gently mix in onions and cucumber.
5. Serve in individual dishes, garnished with egg slices, sprinkled with parsley and sweet paprika for colour. Serves 4.

UNCLE TONY'S TUATUA FRITTERS

3 doz large tuatuas
1 large onion
2 c flour
2 t baking powder
2 eggs
1 L full cream milk
salt and white pepper

1. Steam open tuatuas in water or white wine. Rinse and remove feeding tube.
2. In separate bowl add flour, baking powder.
3. Add 2 eggs in middle. Stir gradually and add milk until a thick batter consistency.
4. Add salt and pepper. Leave to stand 1 1/2 hours before cooking.
5. Add tuatuas to batter. Cook in clarified butter (2 mins each side) until golden brown.

Sweet

There is nothing more impressive than a well constructed dessert or

afternoon tea. Never overlook the potential that even an aborted effort at offering such a taste sensation can have in smoothing over flat disputes and ensuring flatmates side with your opinion. Great 'brownie' points.

Also known to be beneficial in the relationship forging process.

Things

PANCAKES

1/2 cup flour
1/2 t baking powder
1/4 t salt
1 egg
1/2 cup milk

1. Sift flour, baking powder and salt into a jug.
2. Beat the egg and milk together and stir into dry ingredients till well blended. Cover and leave in fridge for 1 hour.
3. Use an omelette pan or other small flat-bottomed frying pan. Lightly grease the surface. Stir the batter, then pour in enough to cover the bottom of the pan. Rotate the pan as you do this, to cover it evenly. Pancakes should be thin, so use only enough to cover the pan.
4. Cook until the batter is set, then turn or toss and cook other side until golden. Turn pancakes out on to warmed plates, spread with butter, sugar and lemon juice, or maple syrup, honey, etc. and eat immediately. Makes 6-7 pancakes.

Variations: Savoury pancakes, filled with mushrooms, cheese, asparagus, smoked fish, oysters, salmon, etc. are not hard to prepare. Make ahead a stack of pancakes, piling up with foodwrap between each one to prevent sticking, and refrigerate until needed. Prepare desired filling, place a large spoonful on each pancake and roll up. Place with join downwards, side by side on ovenware dish, cover with grated cheese or a white or tomato sauce, and grill till hot and bubbly, or reheat in oven or microwave.

PiKELETS

1 cup flour
1 t baking powder
Pinch salt
1 T sugar or golden syrup
Milk to mix
1 T melted butter

1. Sift flour, baking powder and salt.
2. Stir in sugar or golden syrup.
3. Make a well in flour and quickly stir in enough milk to make a fairly stiff batter.
4. Pour into a jug and refrigerate 15 mins.
5. Heat frying pan and grease lightly.
6. Whisk melted butter into batter. Cook in spoonfuls on greased pan, flipping pikelets when bubbles break and cooking briefly on second side. Makes 12 approx.

KIWI BISCUITS

125g butter
50g sugar
1 T sweetened condensed milk
Few drops of vanilla essence
175g flour
1 t baking powder
50g dark chocolate, chopped

1. Cream butter, sugar and condensed milk. (Beat together.)
2. Add essence.
3. Add dry ingredients and chopped chocolate.
4. Roll into balls and place on greased tray.
5. Flatten with a fork.
6. Bake 12-15 mins in a moderate oven.

CRISP MUESLI BISCUITS

75g butter
75g sugar
1 egg, beaten
1/4 cup flour
1 t baking powder
1 cup toasted breakfast muesli
1/2 t almond essence

1. Preheat oven to 170°C.
2. Grease a cold baking tray.
3. Cream butter and sugar. Add well beaten egg and mix thoroughly.
4. Beat in dry ingredients and almond essence.
5. Take large teaspoons of mixture, roll into balls, place on a greased tray and flatten with a fork.
6. Bake at 170°C for 10 mins approx. Remove biscuits with a fish slice and cool on a wire rack. Makes 20-24 biscuits.

CORN AND CHEESE MUFFINS

3 cups flour
5 t baking powder
pinch salt
1 egg
1 1/2 cups milk
1/2 cup **MASTERFOODS** corn relish
1/2 cup grated cheese
1/4 cup melted butter

1. In a large bowl sift flour, baking powder and salt.
2. Beat together egg, milk, corn relish and cheese.
3. Add egg mixture to dry mixture by making a well in dry mixture and slowly pouring in wet mixture, and blend slowly, adding the melted butter as you go.
4. Place large spoonfuls into 24 well greased small muffin tins.
5. Bake at 220°C for 10-15 mins until golden brown and cooked.
6. Stand in tins for 5 mins before turning on to rack. Makes 12.

CORN AND BACON MUFFINS

3 cups flour
5 t baking powder
pinch salt
1 egg
1 1/2 cups milk
1/2 cup **MASTERFOODS** corn relish
1/4 **MASTERFOODS** bacon chips
1/4 cup melted butter

1. In a large bowl sift flour, baking powder and salt.
2. In a bowl beat together egg, milk, corn relish and bacon chips.
3. Add egg mixture to dry mixture by making a well in dry mixture and slowly pouring in wet mixture, and blend slowly, adding the melted butter as you go.
4. Place large spoonfuls into 24 well greased small muffin tins.
5. Bake at 220°C for 10-15 mins until golden brown and cooked.
6. Stand in tins for 5 mins before turning on to rack. Makes 12.

MARVELLOUS MUFFINS

3 cups flour
4 1/2 t baking powder
1 t salt
1 T sugar
3 eggs
1 1/2 cups milk
50 g butter, melted

1. Preheat oven to 200°C. Lightly grease muffin tins.
2. Sift flour, baking powder and salt into bowl. Stir in the sugar.
3. Beat eggs and milk together and add to dry ingredients. Stir lightly, just to combine. (The batter should still be lumpy.)
4. Add melted butter and stir gently. Fill patty or muffin tins, or paper cups, 2/3 full. Bake at 200°C for 12-15 mins or until muffins are golden and well risen.
5. Take out of oven, bang trays down hard on flat surface, to dislodge muffins, then leave about 5 mins before flipping out on to a wire rack with a knife. Serve warm or cold. (Can be reheated successfully in the microwave if frozen on day of making.) Makes 25 small or 12 large muffins.

Variations: The above basic recipe can be used for either savoury or sweet muffins. After sifting dry ingredients into bowl in Step 2, add extras, such as grated cheese, chopped capsicum, sweetcorn kernels, bacon bits, diced salami and herbs, or fruits such as apple, orange, blueberries, strawberries, kiwifruit, grapes, banana, pears, etc. with extra sugar and spices where appropriate. Stir to coat with flour then proceed as for the basic recipe.

BRAN MUFFINS

1/2 cup oil
3/4 cup golden syrup
2 eggs, beaten
2 c milk
2 t baking soda
2 cups white flour (or 1/2 while, 1/2 wholemeal)
3 cups baking bran
1/3 cup brown sugar
1/2 cup sultanas
1/2 cup stoned and chopped dates

1. Preheat oven to 200°C. Lightly grease muffin tins.
2. Put oil in small pan. Use same oily cup to measure in golden syrup. Combine both over low heat, then stir in eggs, milk, and baking soda. Mix well. Do not boil.
3. Sift flour into bowl. Add bran, brown sugar and fruit.
4. Pour in milk mixture and blend very lightly. Do not beat.
5. Fill muffin tins 2/3 full and bake at 200°C for 12-15 mins until golden and firm. Remove to wire rack to cool. Makes 18 large muffins.

HEALTHY BANANA MUFFINS

1 cup wholemeal flour
1/2 cup white flour
1/2 cup sugar
2 t baking powder
1/2 t baking soda
200 g low-fat plain yoghurt
1/2 t MASTERFOODS ground cinnamon
1/4 t MASTERFOODS ground nutmeg
1/2 t vanilla
2-3 bananas, mashed (1 1/2 cups)
2 eggs, beaten
1/4 cup low-fat milk

1. Preheat oven to 200°C. Grease muffin tins.
2. In a bowl combine flour, sugar, baking powder and soda.
3. In another bowl mix together thoroughly the yoghurt, spices, vanilla, bananas, eggs and milk.
4. Pour liquid into dry ingredients and mix lightly.
5. Spoon into greased muffin tins and bake at 200°C for 15 mins until golden and firm. Remove to wire rack to cool. Makes 12 large or 18 medium muffins, very moist and able to keep well for several days.

SELF-SAUCING CHOCOLATE PUDDING

1 cup flour
2 t baking powder
2 T cocoa
1/4 cup sugar
1/2 cup sultanas
1/2 cup chopped walnuts, or pecans
1/2 cup milk
2 T melted butter
1 t vanilla
3/4 cup brown sugar
1 3/4 cups boiling water

1. Preheat oven to 180°C. Grease large baking dish.
2. Into large bowl sift flour, baking powder and 1 T cocoa.
3. Stir in sugar, sultanas and nuts.
4. In small bowl mix milk, melted butter and vanilla. Stir this liquid into dry mix to make batter.
5. Smooth batter into greased dish.
6. Mix together brown sugar and remaining cocoa. Sprinkle this thickly over the batter. Pour on the boiling water. Do not stir.
7. Bake at 180°C for 20-30 mins, until pudding has risen and topping has converted to rich chocolate sauce. Serve hot, with cream or icecream. Serves 4-6.

BEST-EVER BROWNIES

1 1/4 cups chocolate chips
175g butter
1 t vanilla
1 T instant coffee powder
3 eggs, beaten
1 cup sugar
1 1/4 cups flour
1 cup walnuts, pecans or cashew nuts, roughly
   chopped

1. Preheat oven to 180°C. Grease a 30 x 25 cm sponge-roll tin.
2. Melt chocolate chips, butter, vanilla and instant coffee over low heat, taking care it does not burn. Remove from stove.
3. When mixture has cooled, whisk in eggs and sugar.
4. Fold in sifted flour and stir through the nuts.
5. Pour batter into tin and bake at 180°C for 30–40 mins or until slice is firm round edges but still soft in centre. Cool, then cut into bars. Dust with icing sugar. Makes 12–14 brownies.

SCONES

2 cups self-raising flour
1/2 t salt
300 ml milk
1 T butter, melted
milk for glazing

1. Preheat oven to 230°C. Lightly grease and flour cold oven tray.
2. Sift flour and salt into large bowl.
3. Quickly mix in milk to make a soft dough. Add melted butter.
4. Turn dough onto floured board and lightly pat or knead it, with floured hands, to 18 mm thickness. Cut into shapes and put on to tray so scones just touch each other. Brush tops with milk.
5. Bake in very hot oven for 8-10 mins. Cool on wire rack, or wrapped in clean teatowel for a softer scone. Serve split and buttered. Makes 12 scones approx.

Variations: Sultanas, currants, chopped pitted dates, coconut or tasty cheese with a pinch of cayenne pepper may be stirred into the flour mixture before the butter is added. Grated cheese can be sprinkled over the scones before baking instead of milk glaze, or a mixture of 1 T brown sugar, pinch cinnamon and 1 T melted butter brushed over hot scones as soon as they are removed from the oven.

EASY CHOCOLATE CAKE

1 1/2 cups sugar
1 cup cold water
125g butter
2 T cocoa
1/2 t baking soda
2 eggs, well beaten
1 1/2 cups self-raising flour

1. Preheat oven to 180°C. Grease and line with paper a round cake tin, 18 cm in diameter.
2. In a large pan place sugar, water, butter, cocoa and soda. Stir over a low heat until butter has melted, then bring to the boil. Simmer for 5 mins, then remove from heat.
3. When mixture has cooled, stir in beaten eggs. Sift in the flour and beat well.
4. Pour into prepared tin and bake at 180°C for 50-60 mins or until skewer comes out clean when tested. Cool on wire rack and when cold ice with chocolate fudge or decorate as desired.

CARAMEL SLICE

125g butter
1 cup flour
1 T cocoa
1 t baking powder
75g sugar
1 egg, beaten
3/4 cup sweetened condensed milk
75g butter
3/4 cup flour
125g sugar
1 T golden syrup

1. Preheat oven to 180°C. Grease and flour 30 x 20 cm slice tin.
2. Melt 125g butter in small pan.
3. Sift first measures of flour and cocoa, and baking powder into bowl. Add 75g sugar and beaten egg and mix well.
4. Stir in melted butter. Press mixture into slice tin and bake at 180°C for 20-30 mins.
5. While biscuit is cooking, prepare caramel. In a heavy-based pan combine the condensed milk, butter, flour, sugar and golden syrup. Stirring constantly, bring this mixture to the boil over medium heat. Take off stove but keep warm.
6. Remove slice from oven when cooked. While still hot, cover with warm caramel. Leave in tin until set.
7. Cut slice into squares and remove from tin when cold. Makes 12-14 squares.

Variations: Instead of caramel topping, this cooked slice may be covered with chocolate fudge once it has cooled.

CARROT CAKE

1 1/2 cups flour
1 t baking powder
1 cup caster sugar
1 t salt
1/2 t baking soda
1/2 cup undrained canned crushed pineapple
1 cup grated carrot
2 eggs, beaten
3/4 cup salad oil
1 t vanilla
1/2 cup chopped walnuts

1. Preheat oven to 180°C. Grease and line with paper a round cake tin, 18 cm in diameter.
2. Sift flour, baking powder, sugar, salt and soda into large mixing bowl.
3. Add pineapple, carrot, eggs, oil and vanilla and beat well. Stir in walnuts.
4. Spoon batter into prepared cake tin and bake at 180°C for 1 hour or until skewer comes out clean when tested.
5. Cool on wire rack. Once cold, may be iced with cream cheese frosting (see below) or lemon icing.

CREAM CHEESE FROSTING

3 T soft butter
3 T cream cheese
250g icing sugar
1/2 t vanilla

Beat together all ingredients until creamy. If not stiff enough, add more sieved icing sugar till required fluffy texture is achieved.

ARABIAN NUT CAKE

1 cup chopped pitted dates
3/4 cup hot strong black coffee
125g butter
1 cup sugar
2 eggs
1 3/4 cups flour
1 1/2 t baking powder
1/2 t salt
1 t vanilla
1/2 cup chopped walnuts

1. Preheat oven to 180°C. Grease and line 18 cm cake tin.
2. Soak dates in hot coffee for 15 mins.
3. Cream together butter and sugar.
4. Add eggs, one at a time and beating well after each addition.
5. Sift dry ingredients into creamed mixture, then beat in dates/coffee and vanilla.
6. Stir in the walnuts. Spoon batter into prepared tin and bake at 180°C for 50-60 mins, or until skewer comes out clean when tested.
7. Cool on wire rack and ice as desired when cold.

PINEAPPLE UPSIDE-DOWN PUDDING

50g butter
50g brown sugar
1 x 400g can pineapple rings, drained
2 cups self-raising flour
125g butter
1/4 t salt
125g caster sugar
Peel of 1 lemon, finely grated
2 eggs, beaten
4-5 T milk

1. Preheat oven to 190°C. Butter well a 4-cup pie dish.
2. Make the base by melting 50g butter and the brown sugar. Pour into bottom of dish. Arrange pineapple rings over bottom and up sides of dish.
3. Sift flour and salt into bowl and rub in second measure of butter until mixture resembles fine breadcrumbs. Toss through sugar and lemon peel.
4. Mix to soft batter with eggs and milk.
5. Transfer to prepared pie dish, carefully pouring over pineapple rings. Bake for 30 mins at 190°C, then reduce to 180°C and bake further 35 mins so that skewer comes out clean when pudding is tested.
6. Remove from oven but leave in dish at least 5 mins before carefully turning out pudding on to warm plate. Serve with cream or pineapple syrup, warmed. Serves 6.

FRUIT CRUMBLE

1 x 800g can of peaches, pears or apricots (or 3
    cups of any stewed fresh fruit)
1/2 t MASTERFOODS all purpose spicy
4 T brown sugar
2 cups flour
1/4 t salt
1 t MASTERFOODS ground cinnamon
2 T caster sugar
175g butter

1. Preheat oven to 180°C. Grease an ovenproof 3-cup
   dish.
2. Spread canned or fresh stewed fruit in greased dish
   and sprinkle with allspice and 1 T of the brown
   sugar.
3. Sift flour, salt, cinnamon and caster sugar, then rub
   in 150 g butter until mixture resembles fine
   breadcrumbs.
4. Spread crumble on top of fruit, sprinkle with rest of
   brown sugar and dot with remaining butter.
5. Bake at 180°C for 25 mins. Serve with yoghurt,
   cream or icecream. Serves 4-6.

Romantic

There is no better way to impress than to prepare a feast. If struggling for ideas cook something you have never tried before and attach a name and country of origin to the

dish. This can often double as a topic of discussion. It can also appear as though you are well-travelled, thus assisting with the atmosphere.

Dinners

MEDITERRANEAN MENU

Start with a Minestrone soup (p. 34) for cold nights, or a Gazpacho chilled soup (p. 88) for a summer menu.

Pizza - try some gourmet toppings: avocado/olives/cajun chicken/sundried tomatoes (p. 64)

Cool down with sorbet or frozen yoghurt by itself or with a fruit crumble - try tamarillos and apple for a tart flavour. (p. 135)

MEXICAN MENU

Try stuffed green and red peppers as a starter (p. 97)

Then go for a feast that is laid out on the table:

- Platters of chopped tomatoes, lettuce, grated cheese and bowls of sour cream and salsa.
- Heat fillings (beans, mince, chicken)
- Bowl of hot rice
- Warmed taco shells (p. 28)

Finish off with a chocolate cake (p. 126)

COUNTRY KITCHEN

Not as twee as it sounds . . .

Pumpkin or kumara soup for starters, with crusty french bread or rolls (p. 86)

Bean and Beef Hotpot (p. 49)

Chocolate brownies for a real American flavour (p. 126)

GO TROPPO

Chicken satay (p. 79)

Thai curry, serve with rice (p. 43)

Not quite authentic but try Pineapple-upside down pudding for a tropical taste to finish (p. 134)

BLACK PUDDING FEAST

Nothing beats the romance of a specially prepared black pudding. Don't forget the flowers, candlelight and garnishes to create a real atmosphere.

   Remember: My preference is to go to the local quality butcher and have them prepare a Black Pudding for you. This cuts down the preservative content and also insures you have the fresh option.

   First, skin your black pudding, then slice down the middle making two halves.

   When cooking, melt butter and gently fry until the exterior is golden brown while not dry inside.

KITCHEN KNOW-HOW

RECIPE ABBREVIATIONS AND MEASURES

1 t = 1 teaspoon = 5 millilitres (ml) or 5 grams (g)

1 T = 1 tablespoon = 15 millilitres (ml) or 15 grams (g)

1 cup = 1 metric cup = 250 millilitres (ml) or 250 grams (g

4 cups = 1 litre (l)

1 kg (or 'kilo') = 1 kilogram

*note: 1 cup flour (sifted) = only 125 g

OVEN SETTING EQUIVALENTS (NEAREST 10° CELSIUS)

	(Celsius °C)	(Fahrenheit °F)
Very cool	110–140	225–275
Cool	150–160	300–325
Moderate	180–190	350–375
Hot	200–230	400–450
Very hot	250–260	475–500

INDEX